W9-CIH-709

Published in 2013 by The Rosen Publishing Group, Inc.
29 East 21st Street, New York, NY 10010

Copyright © 2013 Weldon Owen Pty Ltd. Originally published in 2011 by Discovery Communications, LLC

Original copyright © 2011 Discovery Communications, LLC. Discovery Education™ and the Discovery Education logo are trademarks of Discovery Communications, LLC, used under license.
All rights reserved.

All rights reserved. No part of this book may be reproduced in any form without permission in writing from the publisher, except by a reviewer.

Photo Credits: **KEY** tl=top left; tr=top right; c=center; cr=center right; bl=bottom left; bc=bottom center; br=bottom right

CBT = Corbis; DT = Dreamstime; iS = istockphoto.com; SH = Shutterstock; TF = Topfoto; TPL = photolibrary.com; TS = Thinkstock; wiki = Wikipedia

1c TF; **8**tr CBT; bl, c iS; cr SH; **9**tr CBT; bl iS; br SH; tl TF; **10**tl iS; tl TF; **13**bc iS; **15**tr iS; **18**bl wiki; **22**tr TPL; **24**br TPL; **25**tr CBT; **25**c TS; **26**bl iS; **28**br DT; bl, br, tc, tr iS; **29**bl, br, br, tl, tl, tr, tr iS; bl wiki

All illustrations copyright Weldon Owen Pty Ltd

Weldon Owen Pty Ltd
Managing Director: Kay Scarlett
Creative Director: Sue Burk
Publisher: Helen Bateman
Senior Vice President, International Sales: Stuart Laurence
Vice President Sales North America: Ellen Towell
Administration Manager, International Sales: Kristine Ravn

Library of Congress Cataloging-in-Publication Data

Park, Louise, 1961–
 Ancient Greece / by Louise Park.
    p. cm. — (Discovery education: ancient civilizations)
Includes index.
ISBN 978-1-4777-0049-5 (library binding) — ISBN 978-1-4777-0083-9 (pbk.) — ISBN 978-1-4777-0084-6 (6-pack)
1. Greece—Civilization—To 146 B.C.—Juvenile literature. I. Title.
DF77.P327 2013
938—dc23

                          2012019582

Manufactured in the United States of America

CPSIA Compliance Information: Batch #W13PK2: For Further Information contact Rosen Publishing, New York, New York at 1-800-237-9932

Discovery
EDUCATION™

ANCIENT CIVILIZATIONS

ANCIENT GREECE

LOUISE PARK

PowerKiDS
press™

New York

Public Library
Incorporated 1862
Barrie Ontario

Contents

That's Amazing!
The ancient Greeks had no compasses or navigation tools. They trusted in the gods for favorable winds and for the sea god, Poseidon, to steer them in the right direction.

MACEDONIA

Mount Olympus •

IONIAN SEA

Thermopylae •

Delphi •

Thebe

• Olympia

• Sparta

Who Were the Ancient Greeks?

The ancient Greek world began to form around 3200 BC, during the Bronze Age, when the Minoan civilization existed on the island of Crete. Through the centuries, the Greeks expanded their territory on the mainland, in parts of what are now modern-day Greece, Turkey, and Italy. They developed cities that functioned as individual states that supported themselves with farming and were known as city-states. Even though all city-states were inhabited by Greeks, there was much conflict between them and sometimes they even went to war with each other.

After a period of wars and invasions known as the Dark Ages, ancient Greece entered a golden age of development, mostly during what are known as the classical and Hellenistic periods. This was when the Greeks founded democracy and developed philosophy.

AEGEAN SEA

Troy

ASIA MINOR

Ephesus

Marathon
Athens

CYCLADES

MEDITERRANEAN SEA

RHODES

The Aegean

The Aegean Sea was the bay of Greece. It was used heavily for trade. It also served as a natural defense because its many shallow reefs and small islands made it dangerous to navigate.

Knossos
CRETE

Ages of Ancient Greece

Ancient Greek civilization began at several centers on mainland Greece and the surrounding islands. A number of these cultures are known as Bronze Age cultures because they developed the use of bronze.

After the period of conflict known as the Dark Ages, Greece grew in prosperity and a new, vibrant culture, known as Classical Greece, developed. Based in city-states on the mainland, but with colonies around the Mediterranean, the Classical Greeks became the founders of medicine and science, and their arts, theater, politics, and philosophy flourished.

TIME LINE

Neolithic
About 6800 to 3200 BC, settlements were founded by travelers, who brought with them farming, animal husbandry, and pottery.

Cycladic
This Early Bronze Age civilization existed on the Cyclades Islands c. 3200–2300 BC. It is known for its white marble sculptures (right).

Minoan
This civilization on the island of Crete was named after legendary King Minos. It flourished in about 2500 to 1500 BC.

Mycenaean
Established on the mainland c. 1699–1100 BC, it was named for the kingdom of Mycenae. A rich culture and architecture developed.

Dark Ages
During the period 1100–800 BC, many Greeks fled because of wars. Most Mycenaean palaces and cities were destroyed and never rebuilt.

Archaic
From 800 to 500 BC, sculptors began making statues of young men and women from stone or bronze.

Classical
The Classical period was in about 500 to 30 BC. It saw great cultural and military achievements. Every Athenian citizen could now vote.

Hellenistic
From 330 to 30 BC, Hellenic culture dominated much of the Middle East and the eastern Mediterranean. The Hellenistic period was the time of Alexander the Great.

Minoan palace
The Minoan palace of Knossos is now an archaeological site in Crete.

Mask of Agamemnon
This gold funeral mask was found over the face of a body in a Mycenaean burial shaft. Its name comes from the original belief that the body was the legendary Greek leader Agamemnon.

Archaic
The Peplos Kore sculpture is an example of the smiling statues from the Archaic period of Greek art.

Classical
The Charioteer of Delphi was made in 470 BC from bronze in the Classical style.

Hellenistic
This marble statue of Alexander the Great, who ruled from 336 to 323 BC, is in the Hellenistic style.

CHANGING CURRENCY

The Greek coin system was introduced in about 600 BC. The early coins were made of an alloy of gold and silver. Later, gold and silver coins were used.

Alexander the Great

Athena

Arethusa

Colonies and Trade

A ncient Greece's colonies had natural barriers of mountains and the sea, which separated them and forced each colony to function on its own. They became politically independent city-states, but maintained trading links with their founding city.

The Greeks set up trade routes on the seas and over the mountains. They controlled much of the Aegean Sea. The well-established trade routes around the Mediterranean made it easy to trade with foreigners. Greek pottery, bronze, silver, spices, olive oil, and fabrics were traded for gold, gems, and other precious items. They also used the sea to found new city-states. By the sixth century BC, colonies stretched from Asia Minor to southern Italy, Sicily, North Africa, and along the coasts of France and Spain.

Trading port

The port of Piraeus, near Athens, became a leading trade center during the Classical period. Here, everything from grains to honey and silver were traded. The Greeks also traded fish, which they preserved in salt.

Ring of colonies
Before Greece was absorbed by the Roman empire, its colonies ringed the Aegean Sea and spread far into Asia Minor and even Africa.

KEY
■ Greek colonies

EUROPE

BLACK SEA

ASIA MINOR

MEDITERRANEAN SEA

AEGEAN SEA

AFRICA

How Did They Live?

ost ancient Greeks lived in houses made of mud bricks. These homes rested on a foundation of stone and had ceramic tile roofs and wooden doors. They usually had two or three rooms, which were built around an open-air courtyard. In the courtyard was an altar, where the Greeks prayed to their gods.

Most homes had slaves who did the cleaning, cooking, and shopping. The women ran the house while the men earned a living as farmers, fishermen, merchants, or traders. When the men entertained male friends in their homes, the women were not allowed to be present. The wealthy tended to buy many slaves to do their work and they looked down on people who had to work for a living.

Women's room
Women had their own area for activities such as spinning and weaving.

Men's quarters
The head of the house entertained his friends in a room with reclining chairs.

Making wine
Grapes were picked, put in huge vats, and stamped on. The juice was left to ferment in jars to make wine.

Did You Know?

Slaves did most of the work in ancient Greece. They were bought and sold at the market by traders from neighboring areas. Some slaves were the children of slaves.

AN AMPHORA

Long-necked pottery vases with two handles, called amphorae, were used to carry food, wine, and water. They varied a great deal in height, with some as small as 12 inches (30 cm) while others were up to 5 feet (1.5 m) tall. Beautifully painted amphorae were made for important social and ceremonial purposes.

The kitchen
Slaves prepared the household's food over an open fire and baked bread in a clay oven.

Inside the home

Wood was not plentiful, so most houses were furnished sparingly, usually with just tables, stools, couches, and beds. Oil-burning lamps provided light. Only the wealthy had bathrooms.

Going out
Women spent most of their time at home. On the rare occasions they went out, they wore their best chitons and finest jewelry.

Staying warm
Men sometimes wore hats and used a cloak called a himation to keep themselves warm.

Women's and Men's Clothes

Etched in stone
Good examples of dress style can be seen on the sculptured female figures that support the ancient temple porch of the Erechtheion ruins in Athens.

People in ancient Greece wore clothing made from linen and wool. The clothing was often very simply designed—just a rectangular piece of fabric draped softly over the body. Most families made their own clothes. Women and girls spun sheep's wool into fine woolen thread, which was dyed in bright colors, then used to weave fabric.

Women wore a chiton, which was pinned at the shoulders and fell to the ankles. Women tied the chiton at the waist and sometimes at the hips as well. To keep warm, they wore woolen cloaks, shawls, and wraps. Men wore thigh-length tunics. Most people went barefoot in the home. Outdoors, they wore leather sandals or boots. Slaves and very poor Greeks sometimes had nothing more than a loincloth to wear.

CHITON STYLES

The Doric chiton, usually made from wool, was folded so there was an overlap of material on the bodice. It was secured on each shoulder with a pin. The Ionic chiton, usually made from linen or silk, was secured in many places along the arms to form elbow-length sleeves.

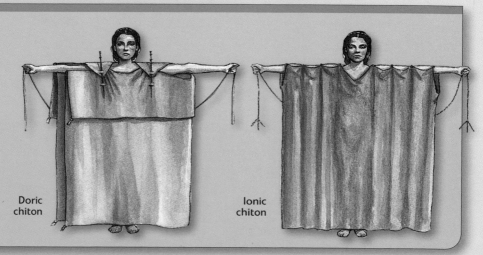

Doric chiton

Ionic chiton

The First Democracy

Early on, the city-states were run by groups of rich landowners. This worked well for a time, but often one man would seize control. The Athenians developed a system of politics called a democracy as a solution to poor rule by one or a few. In this system, every male citizen had a say in the city-state's affairs. Slaves were not considered citizens, nor were women, nor men not born in the city-state. Only men who were born in the city-state could be counted.

A council of 500 citizens was selected by lottery. The council, or *boule*, suggested new laws and policies. It was then up to the assembly, or *ekklesia*, to cast a vote or verdict on whether these laws would be passed. The city-states also had a jury system that tried and judged criminal matters.

Public buildings
Athens' central square was surrounded by important government buildings.

At the assembly
Any Athenian citizen could speak at the assembly. The speakers were called orators.

Marketplace
Merchants traded from stalls in the square or shops in the colonnades.

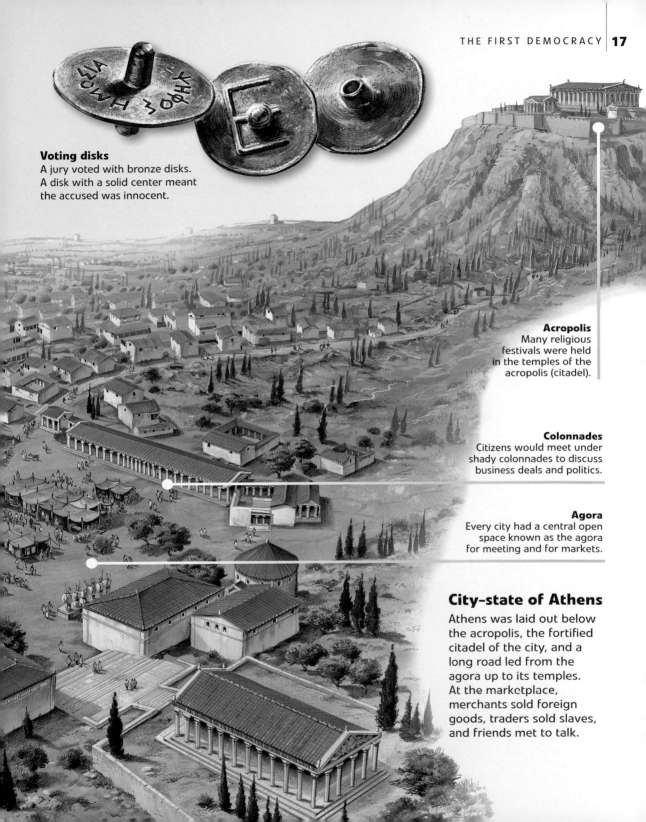

Voting disks
A jury voted with bronze disks.
A disk with a solid center meant
the accused was innocent.

Acropolis
Many religious
festivals were held
in the temples of the
acropolis (citadel).

Colonnades
Citizens would meet under
shady colonnades to discuss
business deals and politics.

Agora
Every city had a central open
space known as the agora
for meeting and for markets.

City-state of Athens

Athens was laid out below
the acropolis, the fortified
citadel of the city, and a
long road led from the
agora up to its temples.
At the marketplace,
merchants sold foreign
goods, traders sold slaves,
and friends met to talk.

Education and School

Education was widespread in Athens, especially for the sons of rich Athenian citizens. They were tutored from about the age of seven in reading, writing, and arithmetic, and later in philosophy, logic, and public speaking. For boys from poor or artisan families, getting an education was less important than learning their father's trade. When boys turned 18, they were taught to fight as soldiers. Most girls were taught dancing and housekeeping, although some wealthy girls learned basic reading and writing.

The Spartans had a very different education system to the Athenians. At seven, boys were taken from their parents to be educated in the *agoge* system. They lived in barracks and trained as warriors until the age of 20. Spartan girls learned dancing and gymnastics. The Spartans believed fitness and discipline were needed to create healthy, strong individuals.

Tutoring
Tutors taught from rolls of papyrus, made from a reed plant.

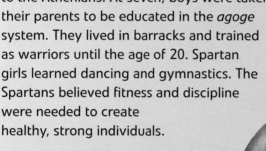

Girls at home
Most girls were taught housekeeping only. Women looked after the farm and home while men were away at war.

ΖΗΘΙΚΛΜΝΞΟΠΡΣΤΥΦΧΨΩ

Greek alphabet

There were 24 letters in the ancient Greek alphabet. They were always written in capitals.

That's Amazing!

In the *agoge,* Spartan boys were starved of food so they would learn to be resourceful and steal to survive. They were taught discipline, fitness, and how to fight as a unit.

Music

A teacher called a *kitharistes* taught music, singing, and how to play the lyre.

Recording information

Boys wrote with a pointed stick called a stylus, on tablets covered with soft wax.

Long poems

An important part of a boy's education was learning long poems, often accompanied by music. They were a form of storytelling and much of Greek history and legend was recorded in them.

Greek Gods

The ancient Greeks had many gods, whom they believed lived on the top of Mount Olympus, the highest mountain on mainland Greece. The Greeks saw their gods as being just like humans, except they had supernatural powers and did not grow old. On Mount Olympus, the gods drank nectar and ate ambrosia, which made them immortal.

The Greeks had a god for every aspect of the natural world and for every aspect of life. Apollo made the Sun rise and set. Poseidon controlled the winds, the seas, and earthquakes. Zeus was king of the gods, and he threw bolts of lightning at Earth when he was angry. Every city-state also had a god or goddess that served as a guardian. For example, Athena, the goddess of wisdom, was also the protector of Athens.

Theater mask
Actors often wore masks when performing in plays. Each mask represented a character in the pla▪

Zeus
God of the sky and thunder

Poseidon
God of the sea, earthquakes, horses, and bulls

Hestia
Goddess of the family and the hearth

Hermes
Messenger of gods; protector of travelers

Aphrodite
Goddess of love and beauty

Athena
Goddess of wisdo▪ art, and war

Ares
God of war

MYTHOLOGY

The Greeks had myths and legends about natural events and unexplained phenomena. Many were about flight. The Greeks thought it a power that only the gods and magical creatures possessed. One story tells of the hero Bellerophon, who captured Pegasus, a winged horse, and flew to kill a three-headed monster.

Pegasus

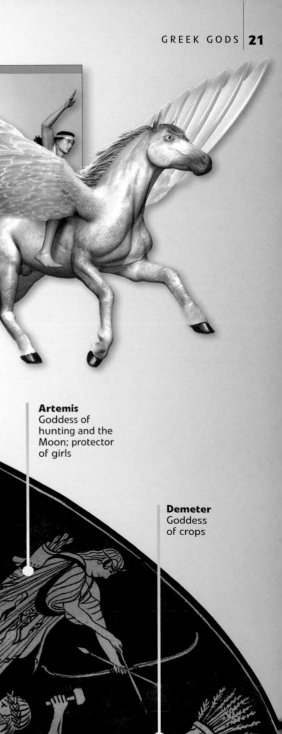

Worshipping the gods

The ancient Greeks tried to keep their gods happy so they would be blessed with good fortune in return. They held festivals of athletics, poetry, drama, and music to honor different gods.

Apollo
God of the Sun, music, and poetry

Artemis
Goddess of hunting and the Moon; protector of girls

Demeter
Goddess of crops

Hera
Goddess of marriage and childbirth

Hephaestus
God of fire and metalwork

Greeks at War

The ancient Greeks were often at war. In fact, it was common for Greek city-states to go to war against each other. The city-states trained free men to fight and relied on them during wartime. Occasionally, the city-states united to fight against foreign enemies.

The army of the Persian empire invaded Greece for the first time in 492 BC. Many city-states from across the Aegean and the Greek mainland fought together against the Persians in wars that lasted from 492 to 449 BC. When Athens and Sparta joined together, the Greeks defeated the Persians. The Spartans specialized in training foot soldiers called hoplites. These were the best and most experienced of all Greek soldiers. In 431 BC, Sparta led the Peloponnesian League against Athens. These two powers fought each other for 27 years.

Armor
Soldiers wore leather or bronze armor over their chests. They also had helmets to protect their heads and faces.

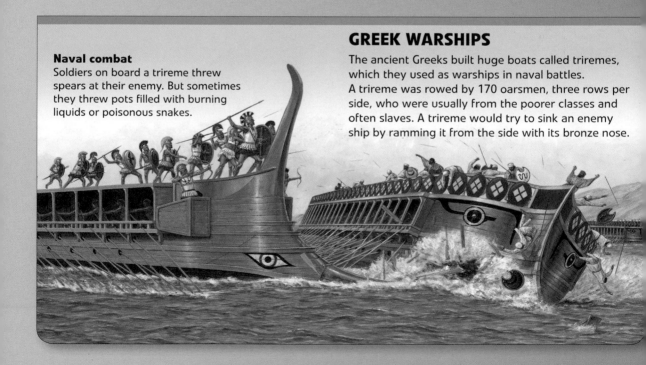

Naval combat
Soldiers on board a trireme threw spears at their enemy. But sometimes they threw pots filled with burning liquids or poisonous snakes.

GREEK WARSHIPS

The ancient Greeks built huge boats called triremes, which they used as warships in naval battles. A trireme was rowed by 170 oarsmen, three rows per side, who were usually from the poorer classes and often slaves. A trireme would try to sink an enemy ship by ramming it from the side with its bronze nose.

The Trojan Horse

In the Trojan War, which lasted from about 1194 to 1184 BC, the Greeks finally defeated the Trojans by tricking them with the gift of a huge wooden horse, which was filled with Greek soldiers hiding inside.

Did You Know?

Herodotus is sometimes referred to as the father of history. He recorded the events of the Persian Wars and described the history of the Mediterranean world.

That's Amazing!

Athletes participated naked at the games in Olympia. Men and boys were present. Married women were not allowed to attend, although unmarried women may have.

Goddess of victory
Nike was the winged goddess of victory and a close companion of Zeus. On this ancient coin, she is presenting a wreath.

Festival Games

The Greeks held four main festival games in athletics in honor of their gods: the Olympic, the Pythian, the Isthmian, and the Nemean. Every four years in August, the Olympic games were held in Olympia to honor Zeus, the king of gods. These games were taken so seriously across the Greek world that in times of war, a truce was declared so the games could proceed as usual.

Visitors coming to watch the games erected tents. Traders set up food stalls, and musicians and entertainers performed. Athletes competed in events such as horse and chariot racing, running, long jump, javelin and discus throwing, boxing, and wrestling. The pancratium was one of the fiercest events of the games. It was a mix of boxing and wrestling, and the only rules the fighters had to follow were: no biting and no eye-gouging. Games winners received palm branches, wreaths, jars of olive oil, and woolen ribbons.

Women's games
Every four years, women had athletics games to honor Hera, wife of Zeus. Athletes in four age groups competed in foot races.

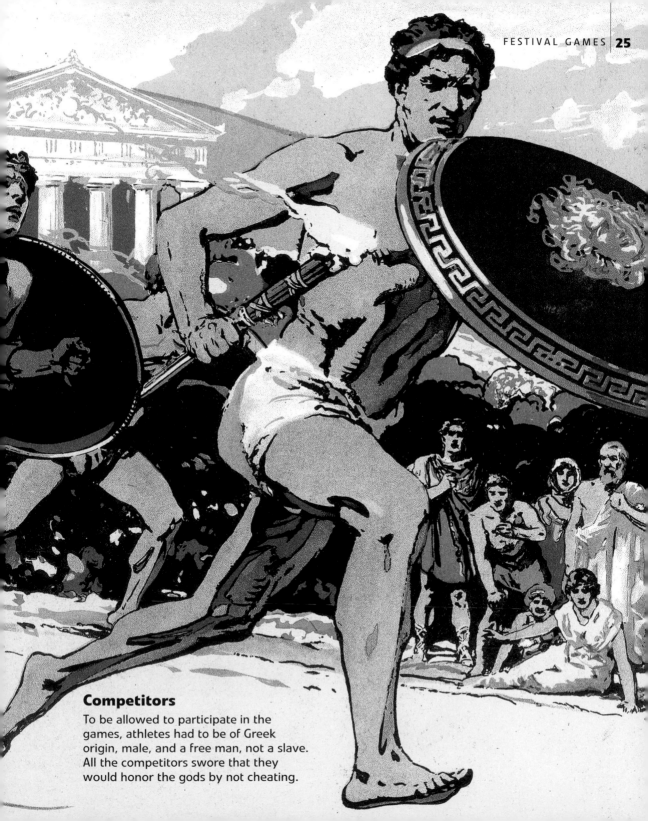

Competitors

To be allowed to participate in the games, athletes had to be of Greek origin, male, and a free man, not a slave. All the competitors swore that they would honor the gods by not cheating.

Legacy of the Greeks

The civilization of ancient Greece has had a substantial influence on the modern era in the areas of art, drama, science, architecture, music, medicine, sports, and politics. Democracy continues to exist in a number of Western countries. The Greek tradition of the festival games also survives, with countries from around the world competing in the Olympic Games every four years.

The philosophy of Socrates, Plato, and Aristotle are still taught, and many principles first developed by Greek scientists and mathematicians continue to be used. The Greeks also gave the world the first alphabet that had vowels. They were lovers of knowledge, who valued thought, learning, creativity, and a democratic way of life.

PHILOSOPHY AND MATHEMATICS

Philosophers such as Socrates taught Greeks to examine the meaning of justice, truth, courage, fairness, and evil. The mathematician Euclid set out the basic rules of geometry, while Pythagoras, philosopher and mathematician, found how to calculate the circumference of a circle.

Socrates
Socrates believed in the importance of questioning ideas.

Amphitheater

Greek plays were performed in amphitheaters, a design which allowed sound to travel from the stage to the very back rows. This theater design is still used around the world today.

That's Amazing!

The ideas and teachings of the philosopher Socrates alarmed some people in ancient Athens and they eventually sentenced him to death. He died from drinking poison.

Famous Ancient Greeks

The ancient Greeks valued learning in the arts, the sciences, and mathematics. This created an environment where discoveries and inventions flourished. Some ancient Greeks made important contributions and expanded areas of knowledge through breakthroughs in their areas of expertise. These included writers, philosophers, mathematicians, astronomers, scientists, and inventors, who are famous today.

War was a part of life for the ancient Greeks and their expanding civilization. They produced some renowned warriors and rulers, too.

Plato (c. 428–348 BC)
Plato was a philosopher who is famous for books known as Socratic dialogues. These recorded conversations about all kinds of philosophical subjects between the great philosopher Socrates and others. Plato was taught by Socrates, and Plato taught Aristotle. These three men are considered to be the founding fathers of western philosophy.

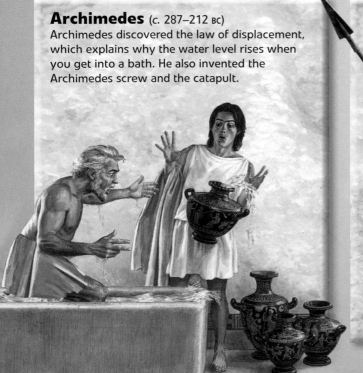

Archimedes (c. 287–212 BC)
Archimedes discovered the law of displacement, which explains why the water level rises when you get into a bath. He also invented the Archimedes screw and the catapult.

King Leonidas of Sparta (died 480 BC)
Leonidas was a warrior king who is famous for leading 300 Spartan warriors against what the historian Herodotus wrote was 1 million Persians at the battle of Thermopylae during the Persian Wars.

Aristotle (384–322 BC)

The philosophy of Aristotle focuses on morality, logic, and metaphysics, and it continues to be taught in universities today. He was the teacher of Alexander the Great.

Sophocles (c. 496–406 BC)

Sophocles was a celebrated playwright. Plays such as *Oedipus the King* and *Antigone* are among the most famous Greek tragedies and are still performed in theaters.

Sappho (c. 610–c. 570 BC)

According to ancient Greeks and Romans, Sappho was one of the best lyric poets of her time. She wrote love poetry. Only a few fragments of this poetry survive today.

Alexander the Great (356–323 BC)

King Alexander III of Macedon, known as Alexander the Great, was famous for his tactical ability in battle and for creating one of the largest empires in all of history. Although his empire was short-lived, he spread Greek culture as far east as India, and this began the Hellenistic period. The cultural impact can still be seen today.

Glossary

alloy (A-loy) A metal that is made by combining two or more metallic elements.

ambrosia (am-BROH-zhuh) Fragrant food of the gods.

barracks (BAR-iks) Accommodation for soldiers.

bodice (BOD-is) The part of a woman's dress that sits above the waist.

citadel (SIT-ah-del) A fortress that dominates and protects the city.

city-states (SIH-tee-stayts) Independent areas where their city is not managed by another government.

colonnades (kah-luh-NAYDZ) Long rows of columns that join to the main building to create a walkway.

commodities (kuh-MAH-duh-teez) Raw materials or agricultural products that can be bought or sold.

democracy (dih-MAH-kruh-see) Government by the people.

displacement (dis-PLAYS-ment) The moving of something from its place to another.

ferment (fer-MENT) To go through a chemical process that turns juice into alcohol.

Greek tragedies (GREEK TRA-jeh-deez) Plays with serious subjects that were written and performed in ancient Greece.

immortal (ih-MOR-tul) Living or lasting forever and never dying.

nectar (NEK-tur) A sweet-tasting drink of the gods.

phenomenon
(fih-NAH-muh-nahn)
An extraordinary, yet
observable, event.

philosophy
(feh-LAH-suh-fee) The study of
knowledge, thought, and ideas.

prosperous (PROS-prus)
Successful and rich in
material wealth.

vats (VATS) Large tanks that
are used to hold liquid.

Index

Websites

Due to the changing nature of Internet links, PowerKids Press has developed an online list of websites related to the subject of this book. This site is updated regularly. Please use this link to access the list: www.powerkidslinks.com/disc/greece/

DISCARDED